SHOW ME THE FUNNY!

finding the humor in everyday life

JEFF HARMS

D1082520

*"A merry heart
does good,
like a medicine,
but a broken spirit
dries the bones."*

– PROVERBS 17:22

LAUGHING IN LIFE

The average child laughs over seventy times a day. The average adult, less than ten. Why? What is it that makes us, as we get older, lose that ability to laugh easily. Is it the responsibilities that we take on as adulthood encroaches? The bills? The job? The house? The lawn? The dog and cat? The cars? The fears we hold for our childrens' safety and future? Well, the answer is yes, yes, yes, and more yeses? And while we're at it, what is humor anyway? What makes us commit to the physical act of laughter? What is the physical act of laughter?

The ancients used to refer to the 'humours' as the necessary fluids that a human body needs in order to remain healthy: blood, sweat, urine and bile. Not a very pleasant subject to discuss, I know, but necessary for us to touch on so that we can gain a little perspective. Comedy was not just some idea conjured up by an old Greek or Roman philosopher, or some ancient standup comic in an amphitheater. No, comedy was viewed as just as important, if not more so, than the serious things in life, what Aristotle called 'Tragedy.' In fact, the last sentence in his book Poetics is "...and now to comedy..." Sadly, all copies of Aristotle's work on comedy, of which there were three volumes, one more than on tragedy, are lost. But the importance of comedy was and is still vital.

Have you ever heard this statement, "It takes a lot to get me to laugh."? Or, "I don't laugh very easily."? Do you know that these statements, however sincere, however believed by the people who say them, are wrong? It takes no effort to laugh. Laughing is an involuntary response to a subconscious stimulus. It is a physical reaction at our most basic, instinctive level. It is, in short, the tickling of our "funny bone" that causes us to laugh. And we call it the "funny bone" for a reason. The bones are the hardest parts of our bodies – the most solid. We don't have a funny ligament, a funny cartilage, or a funny aorta – we have a funny bone. The implication, I think, is that when we laugh, our body is responding at the bottom most solid level to which it can respond. And we can't control it.

Have you ever tried to not laugh when you found something funny? In church? In school? When Dad accidentally hit his thumb with a hammer? Weren't these the times when we want to laugh the most? The "Chuckles the Clown" episode of the Mary Tyler Moore Show was recently called by TV Guide the #1 funniest moment in television history. Chuckles, the station's clown, is dressed as a peanut at a local appearance. An elephant bites him to death. Mary is dumbfounded when, after the shocking news, everyone around the station is making morbid jokes about Chuckles' untimely demise. But, at the funeral, when everyone else is serious, it is Mary who has the hard time stifling her laughter. It is truly a hilarious moment, and worth examining because it teaches us the valuable lessons about laughter.

1) Stifled laughter can't be stifled. Even though we aren't showing it outwardly, we are, literally, laughing on the inside. Our bodies are still going through the same physical process. We want to laugh sometimes at tense moments because . . .

2) Laughter relieves stress. It's the way we deal with tragedy and sadness in our lives. To not want to laugh, to say, "I don't laugh easily" is self destructive. To laugh, on the other had, is actually healthy. Scientifically proven, laughter releases endorphins in our brains, creating adrenalin flow, increased circulation, and a better mental attitude.

I have been performing comedy for over thirty years, and the two compliments I like the most are 1) "My cheeks and stomach hurt after watching you", and 2) "Thanks for being funny while being clean." That is what I'm going to talk about in this book: how to be funny, and how to be appropriate. Humor is good for us, and humor is anywhere we want to find it. Now, not everyone can be a professional comic (although that is one of the more commonly used adages in our culture –'everyone wants to be a comedian'), but everyone has a sense of humor and a bit of wit in them, a sense of silly, and most importantly, the need to laugh. And I think the funniest stuff in life is life itself – everyday life. From our parents, to school, to the signs in the store windows, to commercials on television, we can find it. All we have to do is look hard enough and take the time to think about it.

This book is not a joke book, although I'll share some of my favorites. It's not a training guide for comedians, although some of these ideas could work for some 'would be comics out there; actually it is more of a guidebook for the average person who likes tell a joke or tell a story more effectively. You may find yourself being able to be more humorous as a result of looking through this book, being more at ease in social situations, or in a speaking engagement. This book is a way to have some fun, get some chuckles, make you smile and grin, and mostly a way to... **"Show Me The Funny!"**

~ CHAPTER 1 ~
WHAT ARE JOKES MADE OF?

A joke can be made about made about any subject, but really, without being sanctimonious, why go into subjects such as AIDS, suicide, Hitler, or incest? The list can go on. I don't advocate doing jokes about said subjects. I don't think it helps anyone. It's an individual choice, of course, but the world is too rich with interesting situations and people to "go to the dark side." Make the light brighter, not dimmer. Honest laughs are the best kind anyway.

One more note, There are times where dark humor can be quite effective. Most notably in films and books, the concept of 'dark comedy' has a long and rich history. *Catch-22*, as both book and film, and *Dr. Strangelove*, A Stanley Kubrick film with Peter Sellers, are prime examples. *A Clockwork Orange*, MASH and others are very effective at highlighting the absurdities of war or modern society. Alfred Hitchcock was a master at scaring and unnerving you while at the same time making you laugh. But I'm not addressing these issues here. Rather, this is a book about humor in everyday life, through jokes, toasts, stories and speaking engagements rather than in the other media.

Comedy is tricky!

One of the frustrating things about attempting to be funny is that it's a process rather than an end result. There is never a time when you're 'done' as a comic, where what you have is perfect. This tends to go against the grain of our society. Most of us were raised with, I think, these basic concepts: You grow up, go to school, get out of high school, go to college or trade school or the military, start your career, then retire. Once you've got the job, you hope to improve, of course, but basically, you have the job. You become an architect say, and then you design buildings. But your basic knowledge of architecture stays in place. You might build a better building through new technologies, etc. but basically, once you've got your degree in architecture, you're an architect. Your end product, as it were, remains the same.

The arts, however, tend to be different; you have to learn new things all the time. As a comedian, you practice your craft, and sometimes write new 'bits', while you are performing. And hopefully, you grow. But it never ends. There's always another corner to turn, a new way to twist a line, and furthermore, what you couldn't make work on stage five years ago, perhaps you can make work now, simply because you have advanced in the process.

Now, how do we advance in the process? As far as I know, there are basically two ways – the first is stage time. There is nothing that makes you better at telling a joke than actually telling the joke in public, to people, over and over again. It's very true that we learn by doing.

But there is another way, too. And that is to study the tools of the craft. The best artists are those which God has blessed with ability, and with whom Mom and Dad blessed with tuition to go to Art school! Training in any discipline is very important. **We need the tools, and we need to know how to use them!** And, basically, I think we can break down those tools into categories. In the following chapters, I'll talk about these categories and give examples of each. Here they are, not necessarily in order of importance.

~ CHAPTER 2 ~
COMEDY TOOLS AND TECHNIQUES

There are dozens of techniques, tools, or 'hooks' in the comedy world. I will list some here, and discuss some also. This is not, of course, a text book, so I won't presume to make an exhaustive list, nor will I cover every one of them, but I just touch on these to keep us aware of the depth of the craft. After a while, these become second nature, and as we will see later, they are often combined in a myriad of ways.

Here are some: **The Right Words, Alternative Words, Funny Words & Sounds, Icons, Lists, Callbacks, Reversals, Absurd Juxtapositions, Exaggeration, Puns, Comparison And Contrast, Underplay**

Keep in mind as we look at these that, while there are 'rules' for each of these techniques, we have to reserve the right to break the rules at any time. Thus the fickleness and fun of comedy!

The Right Words – When telling a joke or relaying a funny story, there are three basic facets we possess: the voice, the body, and the words. Obviously, we use the voice. But it is the sound of the voice that is important. Whether we use an accent, or a high or low pitch, a lisp, or the sound of a child or an elderly person is all up to us. We flesh out a joke's power by using our voice effectively. We create characters.

The same goes with the body. An attitude can be conveyed with the cocking of an eye, a furrowed brow, a limp of the leg or the hunch of the back. Again, the creating or even the suggesting of character and attitude can only help a joke's effectiveness.

But, above and beyond both body and voice, in comedy, are the words. The words of a joke are the joke itself, and even though an average or mediocre joke can be made funnier in the telling, by using our voice and body well, you still must have the words.

And by the words, I mean your choice of words in all the parts of the joke: Premise, set up and punch line. And we have to be very careful about how we choose words.

Alternative Word Choices – One of the ways to enrich a joke is by using alternate, more colorful, unexpected or even euphemistic choices in wording. We do it all the time in popular culture. Men try to get to first base with a woman. If we are organized, then we've got it all together; we have all our bases covered, or we have all of our ducks in row. If we eat at a lower end restaurant, we can conjure up a whole set of images by referring to it as a greasy spoon. A bad hotel is a dive.

Old detective novels did it great; read some Raymond Chandler or Dashiell Hammett to get an idea. If a woman had great legs, she had a great set of gams or walking sticks. Even comedians do it. If we have a great show, we have simple words. I killed. I destroyed. I slayed them. I laid 'em out. They were rolling in the aisles. If we do badly then we bombed, ate it, or died. "Why the obsession with violence in describing an audience response?" I have no idea! Maybe the feeling of doing battle with an audience is ever prevalent in the way comics historically looked at a show. I am not sure why we do this in our culture. But I am glad we do. I think it enriches the language. It enhances our connection and helps to add a tone to our intentions.

For example, if I want to talk about something that was unsuccessful, I can say "it was a failure." But if I say "it went down the toilet," then it adds a tone to my failure. Other ways? "It tanked. It went south. Or it was an Edsel." (Don't know what an Edsel was? The name of Henry Ford's son, after whom he named a car; the biggest flop in automobile history!)

This use of alternative choices has gone this way throughout history. One of Jesus' most powerful rhetorical devices was the use of parables; there are over 40 of them in the Gospels. They illustrated very profound concepts by using common everyday examples, such as a man sowing a field on rocky soil, building a house on sand or solid ground, bridesmaids being ready for their grooms, or a son returning to his home. Parables are stories using alternative examples; they were and are very effective.

Here's one of my favorites: we have all heard the term, "mind your Ps and Qs", a saying which tells someone, to behave or get in line. This phrase actually comes from a saying used a few hundred years ago in England. The tavern owners would serve beer in pints and quarts. And when the customer started getting out of hand, the owner would say, "Mind your pints and quarts." He was telling them to watch their behavior, and over time this was shortened to the phrase we have today. So when we decide on the words for our jokes, alternate words are very powerful, not only in the punchline, but in the setting as well. If we get too repetitive in our set ups, then we get boring, and boring is bad.

Funny Words & Sounds – There are, in comedy, words, sounds and numbers which, for the sake of comic rhythm and effectiveness, are intrinsically funnier than others. For example, odd numbers usually work better than even numbers. Suppose you want want to express being nagged by a telephone solicitor. Maybe the line is "this guy called me up ____ times." What number should we use? Ten might work, but we can visualize that, which means then that the degree of nagging isn't so severe. How about "seventeen?" It works better, I think. It's a long word, too and the word teen elongates the sound. Or if we want to be absurd, we can say, "a hundred and eighty-seven."

Not two hundred or three hundred, or even one hundred. But "a hundred and eighty seven" is more natural, it's complex without being busy.
A hundred and nineteen, or even 'three-hundred fifty-eight-thousand and seventeen'. This uses both a funny number and exaggeration.

We can examine places too; Guam for instance, sounds funny. So does Indonesia. Banana is a funny word. Apple is not. It's better to say kids than to say children. Pie is funny, so are crepes.

As we start to get deeper into humor, these kinds of words start to get into our heads. Only with practice can we begin to make it second nature. But it is true. There are funnier word and numbers than others.

As I asked before, I will ask again – "Why?"

The answer, again; "I don't know-it just works!"

And now to take a diversion…

~ CHAPTER 3 ~
THE EXTRA STEP: "WIT"

The first dog I ever owned was a beautiful brown mixed breed named Rusty. When I was Fourteen, my dad took me to the Dumb Friends League to get a dog. Rusty was one of a litter of eight look-a-likes, and what made me immediately drawn to him was the fact that he was the only one in the box of pups who wasn't jumping for attention, paws, scratching a way, scraping the cardboard. Nope. He sat in the corner, looking up at me with beautiful baleful eyes, and I was instantly hooked,

Turned out the there was a reason Rusty was so quiet. For, despite the fact that he was smart, affectionate, and just a bout a perfect dog, he also was epileptic. And whenever there was stress in the air, Rusty would get quiet, and we knew a seizure was in its way. It is a sad and scary sight to watch anyone have a seizure, and terrible too, to watch an animal go through it. So we went to a vet and got him some medicine. I still remember the name: Mylepsin. One pill a day was all that it took and Rusty wouldn't have any more seizures. It was my responsibility to give him his pill.

By around the time I was seventeen years old, I was having some pretty severe allergy attacks. We had moved to Florida, the Sunshine State, and things bloom there all year long.

Well, one day, my mom put my medicine out for me along with Rusty's Mylepsin. What happened next is obvious. Yep, I took Rusty's pill. I, of course, panicked when my mom asked, "did you give the dog his pill?" I said I couldn't find it and she said," It was right next to yours." Gulp.

"Mom, call the vet, I took Rusty's pill. I'm gonna have a seizure.

I feel weird. I feel faint. Quick! Quick!"

So, she called up the veterinarian. "Yes, this is Mrs. Harms. My son took one of our dog's epilepsy medicines by mistake. Should we be concerned? Yes. Uh hum. Mmm. Mylepsin. Yes. Um, humm. Okay," she giggled, "Thank you Doctor."

"Well, Am I gonna be okay?"

"He said to call him if you start chasing cars!"

Now that's wit! And that's taking the extra step. You see, the Doctor could have just said, "Mrs. Harms, he'll be fine. Don't Worry! But he saw an opportunity for humor and took it. Not only did he find the funny, he used it to diffuse any worry my mom might have had. His joke cut the tension, made us laugh, and gave us the answer at the same time. He showed us the funny!

I was driving one night to a show at Wits End Comedy Club in Denver. I was with my wife, Hannah, who was then my girlfriend. There are a lot of shopping centers around Wits End. It's a booming part of Denver. She said, "Hey Jeff, what's with all these stores, Lamps plus? Floors Plus? Carpets Plus, everything is a plus.

"Yeah," I said, not even thinking, "They have a new one – Minus Plus. I can't find it."

That joke has never ever worked on stage. But to this day, my wife says it's the funniest joke she's ever heard. You may not agree, (and I certainly don't!) but it is a good example of how we can use wordplay to spark a conversation. Through exaggerating or underplaying something, we can sometimes make someone smile.

"My date was so cheap he took me to the tractor push."

"My dad is so old, he has false gums." Hannah Rockey

~ CHAPTER 4 ~
HOW TO TELL A JOKE

There are many different styles of comedians, from observational monologist to impressionist to physical to character comedians; literally dozens of styles. And as we've been discovering, dozens and dozens of different kinds of jokes. Stories, puns, one liners, you name it. And on top of these styles, there are all these different techniques, hooks, rules, etc. It can be quite daunting. But in the midst of finding what's funny, of discovering the things in our lives with which we can make humor happen, there is one constant. And that is the way to tell a joke. What are the rules?

Be Concise. One of the emotions an audience or listener should never have when in the presence of a funny person is boredom. Its one of the cardinal sins of comedy, boring an audience.

How do we bore an audience? Well, obviously one way is to not be funny. But the other way we bore the audience is to not get to the point. It's very simple, but, oh my, so many people don't practice it, mostly because they don't understand it. One of my favorite adages is this: "Brevity is the soul of wit."

We live in "The Information Age." We are bombarded by details, dates, the internet, talk shows; they are all around us constantly. And I believe, as a result, we tend to feel that when we tell a joke or a funny story that the audience needs all the details too. But in comedy, when telling a joke, the old adage, "less is more" holds true.

Now remember, you have to be specific in humor. If you go to a store, name the store. But you also have to be concise. I'll give you a good example using one of the oldest jokes around:

"Waiter, what's that fly doing in my soup?

"The backstroke."

A classic surprise joke. Now, here's the way someone who is not concise might tell this joke.

"A man goes into a restaurant one day. It was Sunday, and every Sunday he would go to this one particular restaurant that he liked to go to because he grew up in the same neighborhood as this restaurant and his father would take him there.

Anyway, he would always order the Reuben sandwich. It was his favorite. So the waiter comes over and the man says, "I'll have a Reuben sandwich, and the waiter says, "I'm sorry, sir, but today we ran out of the corned beef, so we have no Reuben sandwiches today." Very disappointed, the man asks, "Well, what else is good?" And the waiter says, "The soup is good today, sir." And so the man orders the soup.

A few minutes later the soup comes and the man immediately notices there is a fly in it. So, he calls the waiter over. And very annoyed, he says, waiter, there's a fly in my soup. What it doing there? So, the waiter says, "Well, sir, it looks like its doing the backstroke."

I was bored writing that joke; how you must feel reading it is anyone's guess! I hope my point is starting to come through. You don't need all that backlog of information. If someone is in a restaurant, we know why they're there. To eat. We don't need a background check on the history of the place. We also don't need that whole other section about the Reuben sandwich either. It's unnecessary. But, believe me; I have personally witnessed, many times, people telling jokes just in this fashion; Information overload. Here is the way to tell it right:

"A guy is in a restaurant, He orders soup, and it comes. He says, "Hey waiter, what's that fly doing in my soup?" "The back stroke."

It's that simple. Get to the point. Cut to the chase. Audiences appreciate quickness. I don't mean to necessarily speak quickly or be in a rush. Take your time, but get to it. One of the greatest of all time, Jack Benny, was one of the most patient comedians ever. He would take thirty seconds just to build up to his classic signature line, "WELL". That one word said so much, he didn't need any more words. An economy of language; use it! By the way, there are other rules we can talk about in context with the soup joke.

Be Informal.   Notice, in the wrong way of telling the soup joke, that I used the words, "A man." That's a no – no. It works better if you use "This guy". Why does it work better? I honestly don't know. It just does. If I had to make a guess, I would say that t has to do with the 'personalization' of the character in the joke. "This guy" implies an informality which, implicitly, provides a sense of familiarity. Also, "this guy" has more action to it somehow. It's the difference between saying, "I decided to go to the store today" and "I went to the store today." It's more active, and more concise.

Lack of formality in a joke can be used so many different ways. Use 'mom' instead of 'mother'. Say, "I flew in today" rather than "I took a plane to get here."

I can say, "I used to teach school" or I can say "I used to be a teacher." Which is better? Well, the second one. Why? Because if I was a teacher, then you know already that I taught in a school. School is implied. It's unnecessary, therefore, to even use the word.

I have three children. No, I have three 'kids.' Someone 'responded' to me. No, they 'said'. You see, whenever we try to economize and be concise, naturally, we end up going for the more informal. And that gets us to the funny faster.

The Power of Three. It's a true cliche in comedy, "The punchline usually comes third." We've all heard these kinds of jokes before:

"This one guy goes into a . . .

Then a second guy goes into . . .

Finally, a third guy . . . "

And that's when the punchline happens. Three creates a rhythm, it helps build toward an expectation. It has to do with getting the reality established by the first two. We then have an expectation, and the third example surprises us because we have a contrast between it and the first two. It works all the time.

Here is an example:

Three old men are sitting around talking. First guy says, "You know, I don't mind getting old if it wasn't for going number one. I have a problem with that." Second guy says, "Nah, my problem is going number two. I ain't seen a number two in a week." Third guy says, "I got none of those problems. Every morning, I go number one at 7:30. Number two, 7:45, like clockwork. My problem is I don't wake up until 9:15."

One of my favorite jokes. A surprise. A built in example of contrast building to the number three, and finally, a concise joke. We don't know the guys names- we don't need to. We don't know where they are – we don't need to. We just know its "three old guys talking." Probably the best examples are the jokes that begin "A farmer had three daughters…"

When the Time Isn't Right – Appropriateness. It might be worth it to take a little detour here. I talked about performing at a VFW lodge and knowing your audience with the implication that you can easily switch gears and not do one kind of material versus another. But there are times when comedians simply don't have the right material to perform for certain crowds. A dirty comic just should not work cruise ships. An older 'Borscht –Belt' style New York Jewish comedian probably isn't going to find his humor going over that well in rural Mississippi. And for that, you have to trust your own instincts, your agent, and the person booking you. Hopefully, you are put in venues where your stuff works. Just like in a personal situation, you have to feel whether that story you want to relate has some merit in front of the friends, family members, or business associates you want to relate it to.

Knowing Your Audience – Timing. One of the common truths about comedy is that timing is everything. This is a cliche. But, remember, cliches become cliches because the truths that they reveal are repeated so often that they become part of our collective subconscious.

Now, let's examine the two aspects of timing. First of all, the performance aspect of timing. As a comedian, you have to know how to pause before a punch line or a sound effect, and you have to know when. In performance, it takes years of experience to pick up a 'comedians ear': that intrinsic knowing of when is the right time.

You have to listen to the audience yourself, the inner rhythms of the room, and be in touch with the many intangibles.

A good comedian can tell when they are on a roll. A roll is when the crowd is with you, you have them right in the palm of your hand and you can take them wherever you want to because they will allow you. You have gained their trust and therefore, they are yours because you, in their minds, are theirs. Getting an audience to trust you is a very delicate task, and one I'll talk about in the second half of this chapter.

But back to timing. When do you say your next setup or punch line? When do you ride a wave and what do I mean by that? Like I said, it's very delicate and it takes a long time on stage to learn and hone it. Bill Cosby once said that it takes the average comedian ten years, at least, to understand what they're doing up there. I agree with this, but with some clarification.

Anyone can write a joke. Anyone can come up with a concept for a gag, a bit, a chunk, or whatever we wish to call it. But to learn how to use these bits or chunks, when to use them, where they should go in your act, now there's the rub. And it takes experience, years of it, to find it and know it and use it.

Suppose I have a tired crowd. Let's look at the cruise ship scenario: I'm on a cruise ship, it's the first day of the cruise and I have to do the welcome aboard show. Here's what I will encounter. First of all the passengers have been traveling all day. They took a flight from, say, Des Moines Iowa to Miami; they got up at 6am to get to the airport. On top of that, they packed the night before, and, knowing they were taking a cruise, they had trouble getting to sleep. They were worried they would miss the alarm, they would forget to pack something, they had to double check with their house sitter to make sure they know when to feed the dog or cat, the mail needs to be brought in.

So, they get up, go to the airport, get on the plane, and fly to Miami. Now they have to meet the cruise ship representative, produce their vouchers and get on the bus.

They then travel another hour or so to the cruise terminal. When they get there, they wait in line with 1500 other passengers all feeling exactly the same way, "Let me get on this boat!"

They get on the ship and they have to get checked in, find their cabin and unpack. Now they settle in. First things first, they're hungry. They look for the restaurants and spend an hour getting lost because of the daunting size of today's modern cruise ships. Finally, they eat, and then decide to explore the ship. They're excited now because the cruise adrenaline is pumping. The glamor. The fun. They have a couple of drinks. Then, they go on deck at five o'clock to watch the sail away party. They have a tropical drink in the hot Miami sun, and watch the ship depart. Then, they go back to the cabin to get cleaned up for dinner in the fancy Four Seasons dining room. For almost two hours, they are waited on, cajoled, bussed and talked to in kindly tones. Plus, they meet their dining partners and enjoy, of course, the legendary food.

They're done eating and after this overwhelming day of planes, trains and buses and boats, they go into the theatre at 10pm to hear the cruise director introduce their staff, and all of the department heads; each takes a few minutes to tell the passengers about the shopping, dining, and excursions they can experience.

Finally, at 10:30 pm it's Showtime!

"Ladies and gentlemen, the cruise director exhorts, "are you ready for Welcome Aboard Showtime?" There is a collective yawn as I come out, and for the next half hour, try to make these exhausted people respond. How is it done?

Now, first of all, I have to have the material. And after doing this for a while, thankfully, I do. Clean. Hopefully clever. But what I need now is patience and timing. How do I 'go after' this crowd? Do I yell? Do I start slowly? Do I try to talk to individuals to try to draw the rest of the people in? Well, it all depends on that moment! It's the hardest thing to do in comedy: Entertaining an mixed, tired crowd. But, if you're persuasive, it's also the most rewarding.

That's what timing, tempered with experience, gives you: the ability to get through to the crowd. Use patience. Wait for the laugh. Wait for them. Don't panic. Stay with your game plan, play the hand you were dealt and most importantly, feel as you go. That's timing. But there's another aspect to it, and that's …

Understanding Your Audience. What do I mean by 'understanding' your audience? You have to be aware of who you are playing to, and what they're expectations are. And it's harder than it seems. And this applies to a professional comedian as well as a single individual telling a joke in a social situation. Or a banquet speaker, or at a business meeting if you're trying to spice up your presentation.

How many different situations have I encountered over the years in performing comedy? I'll list a few: cruise ships, colleges, corporate, nine Mormon legislators and their wives, a prison, kids parties, high schools, church groups. How do you play to these disparate groups? Well, a comic has to know what his or her audience wants and doesn't want to hear. How do we do this? Two ways: we think about it, and we ask. Asking the person in charge what this group or that group likes is quite appropriate.

For example, if I know I'm working a college crowd, I doubt that very many of these students, ages 18-22 have kids, so chances are, they're not going to relate to my material about parenthood. But I do know that they have recently been in high school, so I will accentuate my jokes about being a teacher and add some references that perhaps only they would know.

On a cruise ship, I know my audience is older and often family oriented. So, I might talk more about my parents and retirement and make some cultural references from their era with which I am familiar. I also know they want the show clean. And, to use a common comics phrase, "squeaky clean." No cuss words, no sexual material, and I find the cleaner the show, the more a cruise audience appreciates it. Plus, I have families in the crowd, little kids with grandma and grandpa. So, why risk embarrassing or alienating people?

But suppose I'm not in a professional situation, as most of you reading this might not be. We have to know what's going to work. Three men sitting around telling jokes might get a little more risqué than if their wives are there. Or suppose you have to give a talk in a board room. You might tell a joke slamming the competition that will get a better response than if you told that same joke at an industry trade show, where representatives of that competitor might be in attendance. Remember, sometimes a joke doesn't work. That okay. But what's not okay is for a joke to offend, alienate, or make your audience or listeners feel awkward. Stunned silence is a terrible sound, trailing only a disapproving hiss from an audience. These are the two responses no one, professional or otherwise, wants to hear after an attempt at humor.

Know and understand your audience!

~ CHAPTER 5 ~
FINDING THE FUNNY

There are many different forms of jokes, and the good ones, the funny ones, are not just merely stumbled upon. Sure, there are those times where you might just come up with something that's hysterically funny, and it happens a time or two to all of us. But, as the saying goes, most success is 10% inspiration, and 90% perspiration. Yes, occasionally, a funny idea pops into your head, but most of the time, as those in the humor business will tell you, hard work is the order of the day. Now, it might seem contradictory to want people to find the humor in everyday life, while at the same time saying how difficult it is to find it. Everyday life? "Life is hard enough ," you might say, "without having to labor over looking for the lighter side of it." But, I didn't say humor was difficult to find. I said it just takes work. Effort. And I don't presume to say to people, "go ahead, be funny." No! As a matter of fact, there is a mindset to finding funniness and there are techniques.

Comedy is a craft.

We can learn to knit, right? That's a craft. Probably fun, too, if you're a knitter! Well, we can also learn to be funny, using time proven tools, and along the way it should be fun also! Like knitting! So, let's find out what these tools are. Whether telling a joke, presenting a business plan, selling, or just relating a story at a family gathering, three basic concepts will help you find the funny in life.

The Basic Joke Structure

The Basic joke structure is so simple it borders on the silly.

But, here it is: **Premise. Set-up. Punch.**

That's it, right there. *Premise. Set-up. Punch.* What do they mean? Well, let's start at the very beginning, a very good place to start.

The Premise. The premise is simply the who, what, when, where or why of your joke. It is the reason you're going to attempt the joke. It is, in other words, the subject of your joke. And what can that subject be? Anything you want it to be, but with a value attached to it. An adjective, a judgment, a feeling; anything can be attached to your subject to make it a premise. Let's say, you want to talk about your parents. That's a subject, but not yet a premise. How do we make it one? We add another level to it. My parents are retired, say, or my dad was a construction worker, my mom was an avid thrift store shopper – now I have some premises. That's all there is to it. Add value to your subject, and 'bam' – you have a premise.

From these premises, we are then able to expand into our next part of the joke construction.

The Set-up. What is a set up? Well, it's the middle man of a joke. It's the step we take to narrow the focus of our premise. You see, it's the action of the joke. I'll give you some examples. Suppose my premise is that my parents are retired. Now, I can't really just throw some punch line at that. So I have to put an action to it. For example, since my parents are retired, I can examine the things they do, the places the go, the hobbies and habits they have. That's my setup. Like this:

Premise: My Parents are retired.

Set-up: They eat out all the time.

But, you see, I need something more in my setup. I need to be specific. One of the rules of comedy is to be specific. In other words, if you say you went to the store, tell us which store. If you went to college, which particular college, and what did you study. You have kids? How many, how old, what sexes are they. There are reasons for being specific.

First of all, it helps you achieve to get to know you better. And when an audience knows you, they relate to you more. On top of that, they are more apt to listen to you, to be on your side, to want to laugh at you. It's very powerful to be specific.

Secondly, whenever you are specific with a setup, you may find more information and more subjects to discuss.

If, for example, I say I went to the store, my audience has no idea what I was doing, or what kind of store I went to. Hence, they are unable to visualize, in their minds eye, what experience I'm attempting to convey. However, if I say I went to Walmart, then a whole world of possibilities opens up. Audiences know what a Walmart is, what it looks like, what if feels like. Now, they can go there with me. And along with being there with me, they have in their minds their own memories of any Walmart experience they themselves have gone through. In other words, they can relate.

Moreover, if I am specific and mention Walmart, then I have the option of eventually exploring all of the things that are in a Walmart. From the products to the employees, the auto service center to the garden center, I may have endless possibilities of new subjects and new premises to explore. You see, specificity in setups helps breed new possibilities for premises. And while we're at it, I may eventually be able to start comparing and contrasting Walmart with other stores like it, whether it is Target, K-Mart or a grocery store. Like a pebble dropped in a pond, the ripples just keep going!

Now back to my own set up. I mentioned as my premise that my parents are retired. My set-up is that they eat out all of the time.

But, now I'll be specific. They eat out at Furr's cafeteria, (or Davis Bros., or K & W, or Morrison's). Now, I have something to work with. These cafeterias dot the American landscape, and they are quite often frequented by senior citizens; they cater to that kind of crowd. It's an all you can eat buffet type place, with senior specials and early bird specials, etc. Now, knowing these things, how can I complete my joke? Well, I do it with the simple concept, set three in our joke, *the Punch line.*

The punch line is the laugh getter. It's the hardest thing to find in a joke, and while there are many types of punch lines, the only way to get to it is through that ever elusive comedy muse-WIT! A good punch line is the only part of humor where WIT comes into play. We can learn timing, we can learn how to play a crowd, we can learn how to tell a joke, but the punch line. Ah, the punch line. You have to find it, or it has to come to you. Either way, it's a nebulous concept at best, but by learning the techniques, grammar, and hooks of comedy, at least we can be on the road that leads us to the punch line, rather than wandering aimlessly through the woods without a compass. Back to the joke:

Since cafeterias are frequented by senior citizens, maybe I can find my punch line by using a classic technique – comparing and contrasting. Cafeterias are like something. What are they like? Well, a social club, or a a gathering place for older folks. Like singles bars. Yes, a singles bar. But aren't singles bars frequented by young people, usually looking to meet someone? Yes, but instead we have older people looking for good cheap food. I have my punch line now: I'll compare a cafeteria's older crowd with a singles crowd at a bar.

Therefore, here's my joke:

Premise: My Parents are retired.

Set-up: They eat at cafeterias all the time.

Punch: These places are like singles bars for old people.

Tada! A joke. Just like that. By using two techniques: specifics in my set up and I used comparison in my punch line.

Now, how far can I take it? What else is in a singles bar? Well, how about the graffiti in the rest rooms? For example? You know stuff like, for a good time call . . . or so and so gives good . . .

Well, what would a senior citizen give at a single bar for old people? Not sex, but something else. Well, old people, get? Families tend to deal with health issues as the years go by. It happens to all of us. So, how about a procedure having to do with health? He we go. CPR. Now I have a set up and punch line to go along with my already established premise of a cafeteria. Here it is:

Set up: You walk into the bathroom in these places, and written on the wall...

Punch: Ethel gives good C.P.R.

Now, notice also the name I chose for the woman. Ethel. It's one of a number of old- sounding names. Ethel. Doris. Gladys. Hortense. George, Ralph, Herbert. These names invoke an archetype or an icon. They have a preconceived notion about what these names mean and express to us. Just like, for example, Heather or Bambi or Chad or Derek seem modern, and perhaps sound like names from a soap opera. Specifics. Specifics. Specifics. They matter so much in humor.

Comparing and contrasting. We've talked so far about knowing your audience, being specific and the structure of a joke. Now, we'll start to talk about the actual techniques of constructing a punch line. In other words, the tools of the craft. Let's start with comparing and contrasting.

When you know your audience, there are common threads established between you and them, a common frame of reference. They know the subjects you are touching on, the names of the people you refer to. Therefore, they can relate with you in the reality that you're establishing. And remember, all humor is based in reality. Ostensibly, humor is reality heightened or reality plus imagination mixed with a healthy dose of absurdity.

When we have an established reality for a joke, i.e. the premise or subject, we then take off from that to look for the comedic possibilities. And one of the most effective ways to do that is by comparing and contrasting.

Now what do I mean by comparing and contrasting? Well, it's simple. It's the concept of putting one subject against another. It's taking the reality of one thing and placing it either in the reality of another, or in direct opposition to it. It's a simple answer for a concept that has tremendous potential.

Appropriateness. What is appropriate humor? Well, simply put, it is that joke or situation put before an audience or listener that they can both relate to and that will not offend them. Now, don't get me wrong, I'm not a prude, nor do I necessarily adhere to the current politically correct movement that so permeates our culture today. I don't think that women should be demeaned, nor minorities. But I think we're stretching it a bit when we have to call janitors 'custodial engineers' or short people 'vertically challenged'. It's ridiculous. What's next? A waitress is a 'food transportation technician' or a hotel clerk is a 'human relaxation assignment consultant.' But I can see the reason for it. I think it has to do with the need in our culture, I believe, to treat its citizens with equal respect. To make them feel worthy of being able to sit at the table as it were, with everyone else. It follows the Civil Rights movement when Americans began demanding rights after being held down so terribly for hundreds of years.

Then the Womens' Movement followed, for good reason. And others followed: Hispanics, Asian, the disabled, even since a practice began called mainstreaming, which meant that every kid would have a classroom on the same level as every other child did. When I grew up, we had tracks in school. A, B, and C tracks. A track was for the smart kids. B for the average. C for the less than average. Also, above everyone else was the Honor class for the super smart kids. It made some sense, but, on the other hand, you can see how it caused and immediate sense of rivalry, jealousy and snobbishness. And, to top that, it had the effect of segregating the classes. In other words, there was probably little chance that Honor and A track kids would socialize with the C track kids. And, if we project head, we can see how that could lead right up through high school, college, and eventually, into the job sector and politics. Not good. You'd have a caste system in the United States. (Of course you could argue we already have one, but that's a topic examined another time.)

So, in essence, we've become a society that fears offending itself. In conversation, or comedy club stages, newspapers, everywhere we look, we have to be careful with what we say and how we say it.

Now, like I said before, I don't necessarily subscribe to all of the politically correct mentality, but as a comic, I have to be sensitive to my audience's needs. Remember, the chapter on knowing and understanding your audience? I essentially said the same thing. Knowledge of you audience will create the appropriateness you need to possess.

Now, with that in mind, let's talk about some concepts and subjects that might be in question regarding taste and appropriateness.

When I first started performing comedy in 1979, it was the era of anything goes. Saturday Night Live, with the original cast, was in full swing. Animal House was out. The sexual revolution! You get the picture. But, it was interesting because what most disturbed me was that for many years; my mom wouldn't come and see me perform because of what I might say. There were two things she didn't want to hear: sexual material and cuss words. And quite frankly, I couldn't blame her. If something hales uncomfortable, why endure it? And I found through the years, as I branched out of comedy clubs and into corporate speaking and then cruise ships that those two issues were foremost in people's minds as to what they didn't want to hear. I actually performed in 1990 in front of nine Mormon legislators and their wives. It was a function sponsored by HBO to help unveil the Comedy Channel (now Comedy Central) in Utah. And they were terrified of what I might say. And I knew it. So I opened quite simple. I told them I wouldn't use any language that would offend them or make them feel awkward, and I didn't. And I had one of the most fun shows I've ever had.

I don't relate that story to give myself any great credit, other than knowing what was appropriate.

Now, don't get the wrong idea. I've heard some very good 'blue' jokes in my day, and I've told them, but, maybe in a small group of buddies, sitting around shooting the bull; not in front of a paying audience.

Underdog vs. Overdog.   George Carlin, a comedy hero of mine, once said that you should pick on the overdog. Not the underdog. What does that mean? Here is an example:

A number of years ago, Rush Limbaugh, the conservative radio commentator, had a TV show. (This was during the Bill Clinton administration, but I remember it so well because it taught me so much!) One night he was showing pictures of the Clinton's cat, Socks. "Here's the White House cat." They showed a picture. "Here's the White House dog." They showed a picture of Chelsea Clinton. Of course, Limbaugh acted as if one of his production people had played a prank on him. But I could see right through that. He intended to show that picture of Chelsea. And no matter what your politics, it is tacky. Yeah, go ahead; pick on Bill and Hillary Clinton., or any politician or public figure that has chosen to be there. But Chelsea Clinton didn't choose her parents, she hadn't done anything wrong. She was a gawky and awkward high school kid. And her looks were being made fun of. Limbaugh did a wrong thing. He picked on the underdog.

Now, I know, in some situations, among friends, or groups of like-minded individuals, sometimes anything goes. But, for someone who wants to get an honest laugh, or to relay a good humorous story, in whatever setting, its best to go for the over dogs in society, not the other way around.

~ CHAPTER 6 ~
ICONS

At one time, Dennis Miller was perhaps the foremost surveyor of what we call cultural referencing. Its also called using Icons. Here's an example of one of Miller's references: "That guy looked as surprised as Oswald during the jail transfer." Let's examine this.

Oswald, if you aren't aware, is the alleged assassin of John F. Kennedy. Lee Harvey Oswald. And, on November 24, 1963, Lee Harvey Oswald was himself murdered by Jack Ruby, just two days after JFK's assassination. Somehow, Ruby got into the basement of the Dallas police station while Oswald was in front of dozens of people and on live national television. Ruby shot Oswald, and Oswald died not long after. Now, I know it's not a very upbeat example for humor, but the image of Oswald's jail transfer is so ingrained in the collective subconscious of a whole generation of the American people, that for the purpose of making a point about another person being shocked, the comparison is powerful. And I have to admit, pretty witty.

Notice I said comparison. Yes, that's one the techniques we talked about earlier. Remember: in humor, nothing is mutually exclusive. You can use comparison and contrast along with an icon, or a reversal in a joke.

The use of an icon is powerful. An icon is a person, place, phrase, anything, that has shared knowledge among all the people in a particular social order or culture. In 1999, if I say, "I didn't inhale, "most everyone knows I am referring to Bill Clinton's statement in 1993 where he was running for president, that "Yes, I tried the pot once, but I didn't inhale." It has become folklore, part of the American mindset. If I say, today, "apps", most people know what I'm referring to. There are endless examples for us to draw from. Here are some:

I can say something like, "I grew up in kind of a 'Leave it to Beaver' type house." Leave it to Beaver was perhaps the quintessential 1950's and 60's situation comedy. Mom is a housewife, Dad wears a suit at dinner, he has an office job, white picket fence, the malt shop, everyone had good manners, and the main conflict in the show was whether Eddie Haskell, the neighbor kid, would cause trouble. No one got hurt; no one died or got fixed. It was a scrubbed clean version of America. And there were a slew of shows like it. Father Knows Best, Ozzie and Harriet, My Three Sons, The Dick Van Dyke show to name a few. Some of these shows were very good; I still think the original Dick Van Dyke show is one of the best ever. Today we have icons also, with different identities. Justin Beiber, Britney Spears, Sesame Street (which has lasted forever, it seems, along with The Simpsons). I don't judge these icon's values. I use them as examples because they conjure up specific images and feelings for us. We can then use them to compare, say, today's world, which is so much different. We can plug that Icon – 'Leave it to Beaver' – into a joke a joke or story and it becomes fuller because of it. There are just a myriad of icons to conjure up. If I say, "the sixties" for example, many people will have specific mental images pop into their minds eye. We might picture hippies, tie dye, Woodstock, the Beatles, marijuana, Vietnam, the list goes on. And not only do many people have these images, but many have feelings about that era as well. Now, it can get tricky because you have to delve into that whole concept of knowing your audience that I talked about earlier. If I'm doing a show for retired military people, say, at a VFW lodge, I'm certainly not going to do material on the Grateful Dead, or make a reference to a Rap artist, or take sides with those who protested the Vietnam War. Why make enemies? Instead, I might talk about how appreciative and thankful we should be for the positive things that the U.S. military has given us. That generation which Tom Bradshaw calls "The Best Generation" as the title of his book on WWII. That's a good thing. (My brother-in-law, Tom Donatelli, was in the Philippines with MacArthur. He got wounded. Twice. Tom has a Purple Heart and the Bronze Star. He is a hero. Why would I make fun of him? What's the point? God rest your soul Tom.)

Icons and Labeling.   Now, back to Icons. As we've established, iconography is simply a known name product, even a common cultural reference that taps into the collective subconscious. But there is another kind of icon, and I call it labeling. On the use of an Icon, we're usually using a famous person. If I say, "He walked like John Wayne," then we can 'key' into decades John Wayne's distinctive walk and sound. Even the phrases he used, 'Pilgrim', 'Little Sister'- are engrained in us. How about Johnny Depp's character, Captain Jack Sparrow? I guarantee that helps you picture something. And who did Depp use as a model? Keith Richards of The Rolling Stones! There's an Icon.

But sometimes we can use a known 'type' rather than a known 'person'. That's labeling. Here are some examples:

There are all sorts of types of people out there. Here is one: The Nerd. There are well known people we can consider nerds. Woody

Allen. Bill Gates (also referred to as a 'computer-geek- another well known type). Wally Cox, the late comedian. But sometimes we may not want to name a specific person, but rather paint our own picture. So we paint a picture for our listener of the quintessential nerd. What are the qualities? How about this for a start:

Glasses, pocket protector, white shirt with short sleeves, technically oriented, bookworm, ran the projector in high school. You get the picture, and so will your audience. So we begin to tell a joke or funny story of a nerd who is the protagonist of the story, use these descriptions, and others we can think of, to paint that picture of this person. Rather than beginning a joke with "this nerd walks into a bar", it's much richer if we say, for instance, "This guy walks into a bar; he's got glasses, a pocket protector, a squeaky voice. You know the type." Now do you see the difference? We have painted a picture for our audience of a type of person through a concise description of him. We are fleshing out this character and setting up expectations for an audience.

Woody Allen, say, has a specific look and sound. Yet, often in his films, he turns the expectations of himself on their head by dating attractive women, which is not what we'd expect.

Remember the Hans and Franz body building characters from Saturday Nite Live? Well, they were take offs on Arnold Schwarzenegger. He is an icon. Before being an actor and the Governor of California, he was a champion body builder! With that thick Austrian accent, what a perfect character! "I'll be back." "Hasta la vista, baby." They are common phrases we know. Now, what's great is we can create a label by doing a take off on an icon. Ostensibly, the common, well known image that the media has given provides the ability to use these famous people and turn them into types, while not having to name them specifically, as sometimes is our desire in a story or joke. One of the values of labeling versus icons is that people will just get tired after a while of name dropping or cultural referencing. All things in moderation, as the saying goes. The same is true in comedy.

We can label anything, too. People, places, things. Here are some subjects that can be used for labeling. As an exercise, I like to put a subject down on paper, and then list at least five descriptions that apply to them. It's a great exercise. Remember a very important point: In no way do I judge these subjects by my label of them. Rather, I just label them according to the prevailing cliches that we associate with them. Here's something else: one of the qualities we can always use is to give our subjects is a name.

~ ~ ~ ~

Cowboy
Drives a pickup truck
Has a drawl
Chews tobacco
Wears overalls
Not very smart
Is named Bubba, has a middle name that's always 'Joe'

~ ~ ~ ~

Cheerleader
Blonde
Airhead
Has name like Bambi or Heather
Spoiled
Popular in school

~ ~ ~ ~

Irish Cop
Red faced
Accent
Night stick
Fat
Drinks a lot
Is named Paddy O'Connor, or Matt McKeun

~ ~ ~ ~

Mob Guy
Guido "Two fishes" Monsanto
New York accent
No neck
Cusses a lot
Don't insult his mother.

See how easy it is?

And kind of fun. I think, because it makes us think.

How about places?

~ ~ ~ ~

New England/Massachusetts
The Kennedys
lobster
fisherman
'pahk' the 'cahr' in the 'yahd'

~ ~ ~ ~

New York City

Loud and abrasive

The cab drivers from Middle East

A melting pot

Tough place to live

Dirty in some places; lots of money in others

~ ~ ~ ~

Louisiana

Cajun accent, Cajun food

Not very smart

Humid, hot and swampy

Slow pace of life

Alligators

~ ~ ~ ~

France

People are rude

People don't use deodorant

Wines and cheeses

Glamor and romance

Ooh-la-la type of place

~ ~ ~ ~

Sweden

Blonde

ABBA

guys named 'Bjorn' or 'Sven'

sexy women named 'Inga'

cold and dark in winter

lots of vodka

You see how it works? To label means we have to use stereotypes. And no matter how hard we try in our society, the fact is that we do stereotype. It's human nature. While not a fan of racial profiling, and I pray I am not a racist, we have to acknowledge that there are qualities that we attribute to groups of people, whether they are true or not. Now, one of the positive aspects of humor is that we can, as I said before with my Woody Allen example, actually turn these cliches around. We have, if we do it right, the opportunity to shed some light on these stereotypes and maybe, in a very small extent, rethink them. Don't get me wrong. I don't think comedy can change the world; maybe it can adjust a few attitudes, but I've never seen a comedian change people minds about gun control, abortion, woman's rights or change anyone's political affiliation.

But I do think that sometimes we can make people get in touch with a feeling they might have about a place or a person or era. We may push a button that causes, perhaps, a positive memory of school, or childhood, that they wouldn't have necessarily have thought about had you not mentioned it. I personally find that very rewarding. It's one of the wonderful benefits of humor, to have someone say, "I remember exactly what you are talking about." And, sometimes, they might say, "Do you remember this . . . ?" and they'll bring up another part of the subject that I hadn't thought about. It becomes a very positive give and take that comes from making someone think about something. And that is always a good thing.

Icon Exercise. One of the great exercises to use for Icons and labeling is very simple: make a list of things that come to your mind regarding a specific time in your life. Here are some from my childhood and early life. Some of you Baby Boomers may relate to this stuff.

Etch a sketch
Slinky
Howdy Doody
Star Trek
Chutes and Ladders
Monopoly
Risk
Candy Land
Magic 8 Ball
Pet Rock
Rubik's Cube

Push any buttons? Sure they do! When we concentrate on these things, and others, depending on your age, we think of theme songs, where we were. We can smell and taste and hear and feel our childhood and youth. And guess what: so will an audience!

Limitless possibilities! Because when we compare and contrast, we have the luxury of comparing objects, people, places, philosophies, even time periods. Let's examine some…

People. Think of the many types of people we encounter in our lives. What a rich tapestry God has woven! For example, we can look at cultures; Asian, African, European, American, and then from those sets of cultures we can find subsets. In America we have the Deep South, the West, the North, Hawaii, Alaska. And from the North? We have New England, New York, New Jersey. Let's take New York, for starters. Everyone has a preconceived idea of the quintessential New Yorker. They talk fast, they use big gestures often, and they have a distinct accent. New Yawk. Awfen. They drown out the 'r' sound. It's very easy to parody. Now let's compare our typical New Yorker with our typical Southerner. Someone, say, from Alabama or Mississippi. We think of them as slow moving; we think of their drawl: "Y'all ain't from around here, are ya'?" Suppose we use our comparison technique. Let's put a New Yorker in a Southern setting:

I've noticed when I watch TV late at night, amid the infomercials and real estate, get rich quick schemes, that there are often evangelists on. Preachers barking out at us from behind the pulpit, and starting with Billy Graham, all the way to the present day, 99% of them are from the South. They say 'Freeends' instead of 'Friends'. They are, stereotypically, gray-haired, well dressed southern men.

Now, it's simple. We have our premise and set up using comparing and contrasting: All the preachers on TV are from the Deep South. I've never seen one from, say, New York (Which is as far of a contrast as you can make.) What would a New York TV evangelist sound like? Punch line" "Yo, eh, send me some dough for da Lawd. He will bless 'dee'. Lead us not into Penn Station." (A pun by the way, which should be used very rarely and with the expectation of groaning!!!.) You see how it works? I've put one distinct type into another distinct type environment. We compared and contrasted. Let's look at some more.

Time periods. We have the whole history of our planet to draw from. For example, one of the typical cliches parents use when disciplining their children is the phrase, "Johnny, I'm going to count to three! Now let's take that phrase and put it into another era in history. How about ancient Rome – why? Because they had Roman numerals. And the main thing in the phrase, "I'm going to count to three", is the number 'three.' We simply put a Roman numeral in its place. "I'm going count to 'iii'." Now let's flesh out the joke a little bit. Remember specifics. I used the name 'Johnny' as the child being spoken to. Johnny isn't an ancient Roman name. But there are some we can draw from. Augustus, Julius, Brutus, Demetrius. Let's use Demetrius, and our joke is complete. An ancient Roman parent, "Demetrius, I'm going to count to iii." And we did it by simple comparison and contrast.

Okay, we've used people and time periods. Let's look at another quality.

Animals. One of the oldest classic premises in comedy can be summed up in three words: Dogs and Cats, they are so linked together in our culture, yet as different as animals in behavior, habits and temperaments, that we never run out of ideas for comparison.

A dog, when you come home, will run toward you, wagging its tail, jumping up and down to see you almost talking to you, "Master, you're home, I'm glad to see you. Play. Pet me. Pet me, Huh? Huh? Huh?"

What will a cat do when you come in the house? Lift its head, cast and eye toward you and say, "Do I know you?" Simple comparison. We can take it further. Suppose we look at different breeds of dogs. We can compare Chihuahuas and Great Danes, French poodles and German Shepherds. We can give them their respective dialects as character traits, French for the poodle and German for the shepherd. What does this do to the voice of the dog? How about the physical stature? Think about it! How about something as simple as our pet's names? A typical poodle name is Mimi, say, or Frenchy. Why not give a small petite dog a big rough name? A poodle named Spike or Brutus. How about a doberman named Princess? See how effective comparisons and contrasts are? Here are some more, jut to get an idea:

A Geo Metro (or a Smart car) is like a moped on steroids.

Diamonds are a girl's best friend, what a man's? A dog.

He was so frightened, he looked like a deer in headlights.

Baseball vs. Football (This brilliant bit by George Carlin is a classic
and worth listening to – trust me!)

Cars vs. Planes

Fast food vs. Gourmet food

Mexican food vs. Chinese food

The 50 vs. the 60's (or 80's, 90's etc…)

As I've said before, with humor and knowing your techniques, the possibilities are endless.

Exaggeration. As we've seen, humor is reality plus imagination, or reality heightened. And when we establish our reality, we have to then figure out the best technique to apply to that reality in order to heighten it to its funny conclusion.

When we want to get to a point quickly in a joke or story, which is what you always want to do– one of the most effective tools to use is that of exaggeration. One of the most useful and common techniques in the advertising world is that of exaggeration. The next time you hear or see an ad, pay attention to what it promises. You will lose weight, quit smoking, be happier, meet the perfect mate: it never ends!

Exaggeration is simply making the subject we are discussing bigger or smaller, more or less intense, or more or less important than it really is. We do this because it's fast and effective. When we want to talk about someone who is say, overweight or short or thin or tall, we want the point to be make that these people are gargantuan, or tiny or building-like tall. Heavy people are not heavy; they are 'massive', they walk and break the sidewalk. Short people are not demure; they are munchkins!

When we want to establish a place as having a distinct quality, we want the listener to know how severely hot, or cold, or damp, or unsightly that place is. So we exaggerate.

Remember, though, that exaggeration like I mentioned earlier, doesn't just mean bigger. It can mean smaller. Exaggeration is the way we add severity to the points we are trying to make.

Here are some examples:

He was so big that when he sat around the house,
    he sat around the house.

It was HOT when I was in Arizona…
    One day it hit one hundred nineteen… thousand degrees.

He was so short he needed a stepladder to get up a curb

You see how it works? We simply take the reality – the subject – and exaggerate the heck out of it.

There are some down sides to exaggerating. One is that more times than not, we exaggerate in order to insult. This is especially true when referring to people. One of the classic joke structures, rather politically incorrect now, is the Fat girl joke. I don't know why they are so popular, but again, pick on the Overdog.

There is cleverness in some of these types of jokes, but it is also also insulting at the same time. So, be aware. While I think exaggeration is a classic, worthy technique, it should be done carefully, and in my opinion, sparingly. A joke told alone can have a bunch of exaggeration in it, but when a comedian's entire act is make up of it, or when a storyteller uses them all the time, it becomes both tiresome and predictable, both bad things when you're trying to make people laugh. Tired audiences become bored, and audiences that aren't being surprised get impatient and, eventually, angry. As someone trying to be funny, you must always surprise an audience. One of the worst things for a comic or joke teller to hear is the old phrase, "I saw that punch line coming a mile away."

Also when we do use exaggeration, our exaggerations themselves must surprise. If we want to describe a beautiful woman, we might first choose to say, she was gorgeous, drop dead beautiful, or a real head turner. But that is predicable. Why not be more effective? The old saying about Helen of Troy, "Her face was one that launched a thousand ships", is a great example. We can only imagine how beautiful she must have been!

If someone is smart, instead of saying they are brilliant, or a genius, why not say something like, "He made Einstein look like a three year old" Notice something else also; I must make an exaggeration mixed with a comparison and an icon. Three techniques in comedy are effective and allowed. All the rules can be played with, stretched and experimented with. It's your joke. Find the best way to make it funny.

Reversals and Surprises.   A punch line should have a simple effect. It should make your audience laugh. It's that simple. But, what we are starting to see is that these are all sorts of ways of getting to that punch line.

Punch lines make an audience laugh for a variety of reasons. We can talk until we're blue in the face about these reasons, but the fact remains that there is, for all intent and purpose, something quite nebulous as to what strikes people funny. It's sort of like trying to create charisma, or describing a color, or defining love. It's as hard as defining what makes a certain combination of musical notes pleasant to our ears.

You see, laughter, or love, or music; all of our responses in these subjects are emotional, not intellectual. Now, we can analyze the structure of a joke, or a song and find out, in theory why we laugh or why we like the music, but the actual act of laughter or the delightful feeling we get from music is emotional. As I said way back at the beginning, what causes laughter hits us at the deepest level of our funny bone.

But there is one facet we do know about; our punch line. It surprises us. We don't see it coming. And that, coupled with the unknowing nerve it touches in us, causes us to laugh.

In talking about reversals and surprises, we have to be very careful, because there is both the established act of surprise as a given quality that a punch line possesses, but also a separate comedy technique called a surprise or reversal.

These two words, surprise and reversal, seem to be self explanatory. But, in humor, there is actually a great deal to examine, for there are a lot of nuances involved.

~ CHAPTER 7 ~
THE BEST JOKE EVER WRITTEN

In my opinion, the best joke in the world is made up of just four words. Made famous by the legendary Henny Youngman, it is simply this: "Take my wife… Please."

There is a long history in comedy continuing to the present day of "spouse" jokes. Male comics like Alan King, Shecky Greene, or any number of people I grew up watching on the Ed Sullivan Show or Tonight with Johnny Carson, would do wife jokes. Then, of course, with Phyllis Diller, Totie Fields, Joan Rivers and all the way up through Rosanne, women have based a large part of their acts on making fun of their husbands. Speaking of Icons, Phyllis Diller's name for her husband, Fang, told us so much about what she thought of him and the qualities she perceived in him before she even said another word!

But the best joke of all of them is: "Take my wife… Please."

It's a great joke. It makes us laugh. Why? Because of reversal and surprise, comparing and contrasting, alternative word choices, icon and labeling: in short every comedy craft is incorporated into **Four Words!** Here is how it works:

The word 'Take' is used in everyday speech, initially, as part of an example. We may say "Take, for instance…" and then go on to talk about a previous experience or another car we owned or job we had or person we know. So, in this joke, when we say, "Take my wife…", the next logical step in the conversation would have to be "for example", right? Remember our early rules:

the premise is "My wife", the setup is implied "For example", and we then will expect, perhaps, a story about how this man doesn't like the way his wife cooks, or cleans, or some form of dissatisfaction with their marriage. Instead we get a one word punchline: "Please." The word 'please' changes the meaning of the word 'take', moving it from an example to one of possession. The man wants to get rid of his wife! And absolutely no other word will work. The writer of this joke is really saying, "Possess my wife, I beg you, because I don't want her. Free me from her!" But that simply isn't funny. It has to be, "Take my wife, please."

That's why it is a brilliantly crafted, beautifully concise, simple perfect joke. There are other examples of this powerful technique which, I think, are worth exploring. **Four Words**, and we know exactly what we are being told... Brilliantly! In my own act, I like to use surprises and reversals as often as I can. Most every comic whom I admire uses surprises. You half to be one step in front of your audience, and audiences love if you are ahead of them! They love to be surprised. They love to laugh. That's why they're there.

~ Chapter 8 ~
# MY FAVORITES

~ MY FAVORITE TRUE STORIES ~

Ronald Reagan had been in office less than a year when, in 1981, John Hinkley tried to assassinate him. President Reagan, apparently, was injured far worse than the public was initially led to believe, and one of my favorite stories is that, while being wheeled into the operating room for surgery, this 69 year old President of the United States said to the doctors: "I hope you guys are all Republicans!"

As Pat Paulsen used to say in his act, "That's not a bad line with a bullet in you."

~ ~ ~

The legendary Yankee catcher Yogi Berra is a Hall of Fame player and manager. He is also known as one of the great language manglers in history. There is actually a whole category of phrases called 'Yogi-isms'.

After a game on the road, Yogi and the other Yankee players went out to eat. Yogi ordered a whole pepperoni pizza.

"Should I cut the pizza in 8 slices, Mr. Berra?", the owner asked.

"Oh no," Yogi replied, "cut it in 4 slices. I could never eat 8!"

~ ~ ~

I apologize in advance for any offense someone might take at this story, but it's totally true and since it involves my Mom and Dad, please indulge me.

Before we were married, Hannah and I took a trip down to Florida. I wanted her to meet my folks. Anyway, at one point, I asked my Mom for her 'Blockbuster' membership card. My Dad, in his inimitable New York Truck driver manner, asked,

"What, ya' gonna rent a movie?"

My mom, who was in a perpetual state of exasperation with my dad, said "No, Ernie, They're gonna go film a movie! Of course they're gonna rent a movie. Don't you know what a 'Blockbuster' is?"

My Dad paused for a second, and then, sounding like Archie Bunker, replied, "No, but I know what a ballbuster is!"

~ ~ ~

The actor Edmund Gwenn was a distinguished stage and film veteran whose best role was as Kris Kringle in the legendary Miracle on 34th Street. He passed away in 1959 at the age of 82, and before he died he had many visitors. As the story goes, a day or so before death, one of Gwenn's actor friends was with him and said, "My goodness, Edmund, this dying business is hard, is it not?", to which Gwenn replied hoarsely, "Dying is easy, comedy is hard."

~ ~ ~

Ethel Merman, she of the big, brassy voice on stage, "There's NO business like SHOW business...", married the actor Ernest Borgnine. The marriage lasted 32 days! Borgnine called it the biggest mistake of his life, but my favorite part of this comes from Merman's autobiography, 'Merman': She has a chapter entitled, "My Marriage to Ernest Borgnine". Turn the page... and it's blank!

~ ~ ~

Bing Crosby and Phil Harris were the best of friends, and legendary performers. We all know Crosby, but to refresh our memories, Harris was best known later on as the voice of the bear in

Disney's 'Jungle Book'. He sang "Think of the Bare Necessities," (a great play on words!)

But Crosby and Harris were legendary for two other things; their love of golf and drink. One time, they were on a golf tour of Scotland, playing all of the oldest, historic courses. After each round, of course, they would indulge at the course club house, and then at dusk, drive through the winding Scottish countryside to their hotel. One time, they were driving past the distillery of one of the famous scotch whiskeys, Glenfiddich.

"Look at the size of that building, Harris," Crosby exclaimed, "there's no way you can ever drink all that whiskey."

"Maybe so," Harris replied, "but I got 'em working nights!"

~ ~ ~

My friend Matt Berry was one of the best standup comics I ever saw. However, he never relished the performing so much as he did the writing. He has parlayed his gift into a terrific career: a writer on 'Roseanne', writer/producer on 'Grace Under Fire', 'Ellen', 'Reba', and, as of this writing, 'Desperate Housewives'. He probably doesn't miss the one-nighters!

Anyway, one night back in about 1982-83, when the comedy club scene was just picking up steam, we were all partying after a show at the Comedy Works in Denver. These 'drink fests' were almost nightly occurrences; we were happy and excited to be comics and to be getting paid for it! And it was Christmas. In the background, on the house sound system, came one of the greats, "The Christmas Song", sung by Nat King Cole. I had been imbibing a bit, and feeling both sentimental and philosophical, I pontificated, "Isn't it ironic that Nat King Cole, known for his beautiful voice, making a fortune with these beautiful vocals, would die of throat cancer? Isn't that the height of irony?"

"Yeah Jeff," came Matt's reply, "that's like you dying of rectal cancer!"

~ ~ ~

My oldest daughter Gretchen has always loved language, and it is no surprise to me that she is majoring, and excelling, in Linguistics, and is certified to teach English as a second language. Her favorite comedies are those with terrific wordplay- 30 Rock, The Office, and our personal favorite, the Bill Murray film, What About Bob?

She was maybe 6 or 7 years old. It was Thanksgiving and at our house, I always do the holiday cooking. Just as I am withdrawing the meat thermometer from the turkey, she walks into the kitchen.

"Whatcha' doin' Dad?"

"I'm taking the turkey's temperature honey."

"Daddy," she said, "Um, that bird is way past sick!"

~ ~ ~

Winston Churchill was known for helping the British, and much of the free world, cope with the devastation and fear of the Nazis and their attempted takeover of Europe in World War II. His rhetoric, combined with his cultured British accent and gravelly voice, (cultivated from years of a purported 10 cigar a day habit!) formed an irresistible inspiration to millions. But Churchill could also be a bit terse and insulting at times, and he was also quite witty:a lethal combination.

On one such occasion, Sir Winston was at a party after the war. He had indulged in a few brandies, another indulgence, and being a hero, was holding court and being rather loose with his tongue. At one point, he said something at which one of the 'proper' ladies present took umbrage.

"Sir Churchill," she exclaimed, "I find you quite offensive. Why, if I were your wife, I would poison you."

"Madam", he replied, "If you were my wife, I would drink it!"

~ ~ ~

It was 1986, and the Denver Broncos, with John Elway, were in the AFC Championship game against the Cleveland Browns, in Cleveland. 80,000 absolutely crazy Brown's fans, dressed in their 'dawg' masks, and throwing dog bisquits at the Broncos players, were celebrating ecstatically! Their team had just gone ahead 20-13.It was cold and snowing on the shores of Lake Erie. There were less than 5 minutes to play, and everyone watching, including those of us at home in Colorado, were convinced that Denver's Super Bowl hopes had been dashed.

On the ensuing kickoff, the Bronco's Ken Bell fumbled the ball, making matters even worse. So, with 4 minutes and 52 seconds left to play, Denver had the ball on their own one and a half yard line. So, amidst all this, Denver huddled up. The tension was palpable. Suddenly, Keith Bishop, one of the Bronco's offensive linemen, said this: "Well, we got 'em right where we want em!" The team laughed, relaxed, and then proceeded to make NFL history: the 15 play "Drive", getting Denver to the Super Bowl, and beginning John Elway's legend. Bishop knew exactly what to say!

~ ~ ~

This is a great example of wit and a clever use of language, courtesy of my teenage daughter Anadia. She was 14 at the time of this story. We were talking about her getting ready to start high school, and the talk turned to what she may wish to do some day for a career. After bouncing back and forth with ideas, I told her that all I cared about was that she apply herself the best she could, try her hardest; in other words, every parenting cliche you can think of. Her response? "Dad, you tell jokes on boats: you have no credibility!"

~ ~ ~

This is an example of my wife Hannah's very quick wit:

We were driving through Denver one day, looking for beds. We passed a shopping center, and I said, "Look honey, there's an unfinished furniture store," to which she succinctly replied, "That's because they don't have any doors yet!"

~ ~ ~

I don't know if this story is true or apocryphal, but it is one of my favorites.

There was a comedian named Jackie Vernon. When I was a kid I remember watching him quite a bit on the old Ed Sullivan show on Sunday nights. He was famous for two things. In his standup bit he would do an imaginary slide show of his life; family vacations, class reunions, holiday dinners, etc. His dry delivery made these bits quite funny, and for its time, it was quite imaginative.

His other claim to fame may be more familiar: he was the voice of 'Frosty the Snowman' in the wonderful holiday cartoon which shows up every year. Jimmy Durante narrated the story, and here was Jackie Vernon's deadpan New Yawk accent exclaiming, "I'll be back on Christmas day!".

Anyway, Vernon was a huge Charlie Chaplin fan. He just about worshiped him, as did many people in the entertainment world.

Show Me The Funny!

Chaplin was an extraordinary genius, yet had quite a troubled personal life. His foibles eventually made him leave America, and move to France. Jackie Vernon began writing letters to Chaplin at a very young age. The type of fan letters where he would explain how he wanted to be a comedian someday, how Chaplin was his inspiration and hero. He would write these letters religiously, month after month, for years. He never heard back from Chaplin, not even a publicity picture, and eventually gave up.

Many years later, after Jackie Vernon had become well known and well off, he was invited to attend a gala in honor of Chaplin's triumphant return, at age 80, to America to be honored at the Academy awards. It was, understandably, a huge deal! There are hundreds of luminaries, all in their finest, waiting in line for a brief introduction with the legend At last Jackie Vernon comes face to face with his hero. He is introduced, and it is explained to Chaplin that Jackie Vernon is a very well known and successful American comic. Chaplin paused a moment, looked at him and said, "Jackie Vernon! Why did you stop writing?" CLASSIC!

~ ~ ~

Parents of young children should relate to this story. When my son Chris was about 4 years old, the most difficult part of the day was to get him to go to bed. He had a play instinct and an energy unmatched by any other child I have ever seen. One night, after getting him washed up and in his pajamas, he wanted to play some more. I kept after him; it was well after 11:00 P.M, and he showed no sign of slowing down. Finally, after losing patience, I raised my voice, "Chris, bedtime NOW!" Looking at me defiantly, he said the most logical thing that can come to a 4 year old's brain: "Fine:I'll sleep all night then!!!"

1) A man walks into a bar. He orders 10 shots of whiskey. The bartender pours all ten shots, and the man proceeds to down all of them without a break.

"My goodness", the bartender says, "How can you drink like that?"

"Let me tell you something," the man slurs, "if you had what I had, you would drink like that too."

"Oh…really", the bartender says. "What do you have?"

"Fifty cents."

2) A man calls up his friend. His friend's 7 year old son answers the phone and whispering, says,

"Hello."

"Hi. Is your dad there?"

"Yeah, but he's busy."

"Is your Mom there?"

"Yeah, but she's busy too."

"Where's your older brother?"

"Busy."

"Older sister."

(Adamantly whispering) "Busy. everybody's busy."

"What's everybody doing?"

"Lookin' for me!"

3) **An old man says to his best friend, "you know, I've known you my whole life, and so help me, I can't remember your name." His friend looks at him for a moment and says, "How soon do you need it?"**

4) Two very old couples are chatting. One of the men says, "You know, we had dinner the other night-best place in years." His friend says, "What was the name of it?" His friend suddenly draws an absolute blank. "Um....think of a flower."

"Daisy?"

"No, think of another flower."

"Tulip?"

"No. Think of another one."

"Rose?"

He turns to his wife, "Rose, what was the name of that restaurant...?"

5) The man who wrote the song 'The Hokey Pokey' died yesterday at age 93. It took them 11 hours to get him in the casket: "You put the right one in, you pull the right one out..."

~ FIVE OF MY FAVORITE 'PG-13' JOKES ~

1) A farmer has three daughters. One Friday night he's sitting at home. There's a knock on his door, he answers and there's a guy standing there.

"Who are you?"

"Hi. I'm Eddy, I'm here for Betty. We're goin' for spaghetti. She ready?"

The farmer calls Betty, and she and the man leave. He sits back down. Another knock.

"Who are you?"

"Hi. I'm Joe. I'm here for Flo. We're goin' to the show. She ready to go?"

The farmer calls Flo. They leave.

He sits back down, and of course, a third knock.

"Who are you?"

"Hi. I'm Chuck."

And the farmer shot him!

2) It's a wedding night in a honeymoon suite, and a very pure, virginal newlywed couple are looking at each other. Finally the groom says,

"Honey would you do me one favor before anything else happens?"

"Anything," she replies, "I'm now you're wife. Anything."

"Good." He proceeds to take off his trousers. "Would you put these on?"

"Okay," she says. She puts on his pants, and they are just hanging off of her, they are so loose.

"Um, I can't wear these pants."

    "That's right", her husband says. "And I want you to remember who wears the pants in this marriage."

She then says, "Would you do me a favor?"

"Anything."

She takes off her panties. "Here put these on."

He puts them on and he can only get them up to his knees.

"I can't get into these panties."

"That's right', she replies, "and you're not gonna unless your attitude changes!"

3) Man and wife asleep in bed at 3 in the morning. The phone rings. The man grouchily answers.

"Hello? What? How am I supposed to know that? That's like 1200 miles away! Call the Navy." He slams the phone down.

"Who was that?" his wife asks.

"Some idiot who wants to know if the coast is clear!"

4) Two good friends are playing golf. Up ahead are two women playing very slowly. One of the guys says,

"I'm gonna go ask those ladies if we can play through."

He leaves, gets halfway and turns around.

"What's the matter?", his friend says.

"I can't talk to those women. One is my wife, and the other is this woman I been running around with on the side!"

"I'll go," his friend says. He leaves. He gets halfway, turns around and comes running back.

"Wow, small world isn't it?"

5) Three presidents, Jimmy Carter, Richard Nixon and Bill Clinton, are on a ship in Alaska. The ship hits an iceberg and starts to sink.

Jimmy Carter says, "Save the women first."

Nixon says, "Screw the women."

Bill Clinton says, "You think we have time?"

"Wagner's music is better than it sounds."
– Mark Twain

"The rumors of my death are greatly exaggerated."
– Mark Twain

"All in all, I'd rather be here than in Philadelphia."
– W.C. Fields – on his gravestone!

"90 percent of baseball is half-mental."
– Yogi Berra

"I feel sorry for people who don't drink, because when they wake up in the morning, that's as good as they're gonna feel all day."
– Lenny Bruce

"There are three types of people in the world: those who understand math, and those that don't."
– Anonymous

"I don't believe in an afterlife-although I am bringing
a change of underwear."
– Woody Allen

"I went jogging today. I pulled a groin muscle; it wasn't mine!
He gave me a number; it wasn't his."
– Hannah Rockey

"The problem with Italian food is two or three days later
you're hungry again."
– Anonymous

"The curtain came up at 8 o'clock sharp and
went down at 10 o'clock dull."
– Dorothy Parker

"George Bush was born with a silver foot in his mouth."
– Ann Richards

It may seem odd to equate humor with Christianity, or for that matter, with any kind of spiritual sense at all. We are raised to think that God is housed in a place of hushed, somber tones, organ music, choir robes and stained glass, or folk hymns are being played by a group of well-scrubbed folk singers in jeans, and comedy consists of clean cut humor spun from stories about 'granny', down home on the farm in small town America, or cute ventriloquist dolls telling silly stories. Both of these kinds of atmospheres are fine with me, thank you very much, and I am in no way denigrating them. However, I believe, as a Christian, there is so much more to offer artistically.

First of all, I am not talking about using a Christian approach to comedy to further a political agenda. In my opinion, the most dangerous area a comic can go to is that area where he/she feels that what they say is 'important' or 'profound', whether they are religious or not. There are a number of pitfalls with this:

To begin with, in most cases you are preaching to the choir. I remember in 1992 when the first Gulf War began, and a lot of comedians were, basically, becoming 'rabble rousers'. They would call Arabs 'towel-heads', and use this jingoism as an easy way to get cheers. Conversely, it's awfully easy to rail against the current administration in power, be they Democrat or Republican . I enjoy some political satire; Saturday Nite Live, the now defunct Mad-TV, and John Stewart and Steven Colbert are great examples of political humor done well. But there is a reason for this. They use a long form style; they do sketches, they have a team of people around them acting as writers and 'correspondents', and they have guests. Most importantly, they point our the foibles and absurdities we witness so often from, as George Carlin used to call them, the 'Overdogs'.

But the danger with performing political humor in a live setting as a standup is that often you lose sight of the fact that you are a comedian, and that your job is to make people laugh. The road to 'not-being-funny' is strewn with comedians who started to take themselves, and their political opinions, way too seriously: Dennis Miller has become a really bad punster shill for Bill O'Reilly. George Carlin spent the last 10 years of his brilliant career just standing on stage and name calling and complaining against easy targets-golfers, business people, you name it, he made fun of it. The problem? It wasn't funny. Bill Maher; here's another example of a comic who was very funny and now thinks he is 'important'. He started with 'Politically Incorrect', got canceled by ABC after saying that the 9/11 terrorists, while having done a despicable thing, were not cowards.(Whether they were justified uin firing him is not for this book!) He then landed on HBO, where he still has a weekly show called 'Real Time'. He has a lively roundtable discussion about issues of the day, using a variety of guests, and most times it's fun. But the least entertaining part of his show is his monologue. He tends to be pedantic and preachy.

Don't get me wrong. There is a rich tradition of political humor in America. Will Rogers. Doonesbury. Hunter S. Thompson. Mark Twain. Johnny Carson's opening monologue for thirty years often had social commentary. I had the tremendous honor of opening for Mort Sahl in Denver a number of years ago, and he would stand on stage with the newspaper and make brilliant observations on the events of the day. It was great, and by the way, Mort Sahl is one of the nicest human beings I have ever met-in or out of show business, along with George Carlin!

But these people really know their audiences, they really know that they needed to be funny and they knew when to back off. They didn't beat any dead horses.

Another problem with modern political humor is simply that there is not a great deal of credibility among those who purport to be profound. We are talking comics, for goodness sake! We are not political scientists, we are men and women who can twist a phrase and come up with punchlines. As my friend Todd Jordan once said to a young comic who said he wanted to talk about 'important' things, "You sit on your butt in a condo all day watching MTV and eating fast food; and you think that that gives your half hour in a bar reason to be political?" He was right. So I think I have established that we don't need Christian comics to be political.

I also don't think we need Christian comics to preach. You know who does that? Preachers. I believe that we are there to entertain, but we are to do it in a positive way. But then, what does that mean? Motivational speaking? The power of 'believing, conceiving and receiving' and other such psycho-babble? Nah! Here's what I mean:

If you look through the New Testament, particularly those books called the Epistles, (not the four Gospels, Acts, or Revelation; but the letters of instruction written by Paul, Peter, John, James and Jude), you might notice what I like to call the 'lists'. These are instructions on how to feel and think, and how to perceive the world through the eyes of a believer. Here is one example:

In the book of Galatians, the apostle Paul says that "...the acts of the flesh are...sexual immorality, impurity and debauchery; idolatry and witchcraft; hatred, discord, jealousy, fits of rage, selfish ambition. dissensions, factions and envy; drunkenness, orgies and the like." (5:19-21)

I would say that these are truly unpleasant and undesirable practices in which to live our lives. In any case, so much of our popular culture has become defined by the very things which Paul wrote about 2000 years ago. We actually celebrate some of this stuff!

However, Paul never gives a negative reading of humanity without offering the opposite, positive, Spirit-filled alternative. Here's what he says next: "But the fruit of the Spirit is love, joy, peace, forbearance (patience), kindness, goodness, faithfulness, gentleness and self-control." (Galatians 5:22-23)

Do you notice the very subtle differences in the types, or 'manners' with which Paul instructs. The negative are acts, while the positive are attributes. This may sound like splitting hairs, but it is tremendously important in my opinion. We are told how not to behave; but we are also instructed how to be. How does this relate to comedy? Well, for one thing, the act of laughter itself creates a positive response in the chemicals in our body. I believe that most people would rather laugh at something that makes them feel good, or positive, or kind, rather than that which is at the expense of someone's well-being, or their mistake, or their misfortune. There is an old comedy cliche: if it bends it's funny, if it breaks, it's not funny. Silly, I know, but true. Let us keep that in mind.

We need to remember that 'a merry heart does good, like a medicine.' Jesus had a merry heart. He is the source of all joy. He wept. He felt compassion, and He could be angry. But we forget that one of the first things we have recorded in the Gospels of him saying is a pun. What did He say to the fishermen? "Follow me, and I will make you fishers of men." Not bad. Not bad at all.

Tastes in comedy and what makes us laugh are totally subjective. So, for what it's worth, here's a list of some of my favorite comedy things: books, films, people, whatever. Again, totally subjective, and nowhere near exhaustive.

Young Frankenstein, Animal House. Anything with Bill Murray, Gene Wilder, The Marx Brothers, Abbott and Costello (up to and including '… Meet Frankenstein),(Who's on First is the greatest comedy routine. EVER!) Laurel and Hardy; and for men only, The Three Stooges, but only with Curly or Shemp.

Jackie Gleason, (on TV, not movies except for two unknown gems; 'Gigot' and 'Soldier in the Rain', a great movie with Steve McQueen!), Carol Burnett's show, Dick Van Dyke's original show and Mary Tyler Moore's too. Anything with Bob Newhart, The Office, both British and American. 30 Rock, where Alec Baldwin's performance will go down as one of the greats! The Andy Griffith Show, but only the first 5 seasons, with the astounding Don Knotts; watch him try to remember the Declaration of Independence, and not laugh! The Little Rascals, especially with Alfalfa singing; The Beatles in 'A Hard Day's Night'; in 'Help', watch John Lennon quiz the Scotland Yard guy about jack the Ripper! The first 6 seasons of 'Seinfeld'. Bert Lahr in 'The Wizard of Oz'.

Extras on HBO, Monty Python's movies, Dudley Moore and Peter Cook's one legged man sketch and 'Peach and Frog'; Chevy Chase in 'Fletch' and 'Funny Farm', and especially the 'Vacation' movies.

Woody Allen's two books 'Without Feathers' and 'Getting Even', along with his 'early funny' movies.

Johnny Carson-always! Letterman, Ferguson, Kimmel, Leno, Maher; all in small doses. Chris Rock and Dave Chappelle in concert movies. Dom Irerrera, Brian Regan, Paula Poundstone. Don Rickles. Jack Benny. Burns and Allen. Old radio shows. Hope and Crosby movies; I saw Bob Hope in concert when he was 75-brilliant! Marlon Brando and David Niven in 'Bedtime Story', later made into 'Dirty Rotten scoundrels' with Michael Caine and Steve Martin. Steve Martin! Brando in 'The Freshman', 'The Birdcage', Kristen Wiig on SNL.

Dean Martin's variety show; Jerry Lewis in 'The Nutty Professor',(Eddie Murphy's remake too!) 'Hook, Line and Sinker', and Martin Short's impression of him; John Byner's impression of John Wayne as a priest! Joan Rivers, Totie Fields, Robert Shimmel (God rest his soul), 'Arrested Development', Chris Farley.

There are hundreds more that make me laugh. I can't begin to tell you how much laughter means to all of us, but this list is a start; add to it, and enjoy.

~ CONCLUSION ~

This is not a deep book on comedy. Rather, my purpose is to let people get their feet wet a bit in the comedy swimming pool. You will find, whether it is in a comedy club, at a banquet, in a talent show, or just at a gathering of family and friends, that the water is fine. Give it a shot. Comedy is fun, and there is something rewarding about creating something which people appreciate. Try to be funny. It's fun, What have you got to lose? Like I always tell my students, "Nobody's gonna laugh at you!"

Thanks. You've been great. Enjoy the veal!

Jeff Harms

my email: jharmscomic@yahoo.com

my agent: Ken Muller's Comedy Productions

ken@comedypro.com 712-276-3035

~ ACKNOWLEDGMENTS ~

I would like to acknowledge many people who have taught me through the years, but space doesn't permit. Suffice it to say the following: my family, kids, friends and fellow comics. Specifically, however, thanks to David Ball and C.H. Rockey for their help with the production of this book, to George, Ken, my sister who always makes me laugh *(especially on birthdays!)*, Ralph Achilles, Chris, Gretchen, Anadia, and finally, my best friend and the coolest person I know – the funniest and bravest too – my wife Hannah. I like her a lot! And of course, The Lord above, who was, is and always will be.